THE MYSTERY OF ORDINANCES

How To Understand The Mysteries Of God

Linda E. Akassa Lakemfa

ISBN: 9798840208199

All Scriptures quoted are from King James Version of the Bible except otherwise stated.

SEVEN ORDINANCES OF FAVOUR

CHAPTER 1

THE MYSTERY OF ORDINANCES

God is a God of mystery; He rides on the wings of the wind. He is deep, his ways are also deep. He is all-knowing, even though no one can know him in all of His totality; therefore, life operates on both the revealed and unrevealed truth.

For this cause I Paul, the prisoner of Jesus Christ for you Gentiles,
If ye have heard of the dispensation of the grace of God which is given me to you-ward:
How that by revelation he made known unto me the mystery; (as I wrote afore in few words,
Whereby, when ye read, ye may understand my knowledge in the mystery of Christ)
Which in other ages was not made known unto the sons of men, as it is now revealed unto his holy apostles and prophets by the Spirit; Ephesians 3:1-5.

And to make all men see what is the fellowship of the mystery, which from the beginning of the world hath been hid in God, who created all things by Jesus Christ: Ephesians 3:9.

And without controversy great is the mystery of godliness: God was manifest in the flesh, justified in the Spirit, seen of angels, preached unto the Gentiles, believed on in the world, received up into glory. 1Tm:3:16

The grace of our Lord Jesus Christ be with you all. Amen.
Now to him that is of power to stablish you according to my gospel, and the preaching of Jesus Christ, according to the revelation of the mystery, which was kept secret since the world began,

But now is made manifest, and by the scriptures of the prophets, according to the commandment of the everlasting God, made known to all nations for the obedience of faith Romans16:24-26

Mysteries of God are spiritual truths known only by revelation and must be handle with clear conscience. The mystery of God comes with comfort when we acknowledge with clear conscience.

Holding the mystery of the faith in a pure conscience. 1Tm:3:9

That their hearts might be comforted, being knit together in love, and unto all riches of the full assurance of understanding, to the acknowledgement of the mystery of God, and of the Father, and of Christ;
In whom are hid all the treasures of wisdom and knowledge. Colossian 2:2-3

God reveals His mysteries to those who follow Him and whosoever He decided to reveals them to. There is more about God's mysteries yet to be unveiled to man than humanity has ever experienced.

It is given unto you to know the mysteries of the kingdom of heaven, Matthew 13:11.

What is an ordinance: An ordinance is a religious practice prescribed by the church as directed by the Holy Spirit.
An ordinance is the physical act of divine instruction of that which is spiritually aimed to bring about the manifestation of the supernatural and making tangible that which is of the spirit. It is acting out physically that which is seen in the spirit's realm. It is a physical practice of a divine instruction
An ordinance is an outward expression of the invisible sign to bring about a divine manifestation of God's grace.
Ordinances are heavenly instructions carried out on the earth to secure the backing of heaven.

They continue this day according to thine ordinances: for all are thy servants. Psalm 119:91.

The Bible as seen in the above reference state thus; they continue this day according to thine ordinances". Because the Lord has bid the universe to abide, therefore it stands, and all its laws continue to operate with precision and power. Because the might of God is ever-present to maintain them, therefore, all things continue. The word which spoke all things into existence has supported them till now, and still supports them both in being and in well-being. God's ordinance is the reason for the continued existence of creation. What important forces these ordinances are! "For all are thy servants." Created by thy word, they obey that word, thus answering the purpose of their existence, and working out the design of their Creator. Great things and small, pay homage to the Lord. No atom escapes his rule, no world avoids his government. Shall we wish to be free of the Lord's way and become lords unto ourselves? If we were so, we should be dreadful exceptions to a law that secures the well-being of the universe. Rather, while we read concerning all things else, they continue and they serve. Let us continue to serve, and to serve more perfectly as our lives continued. By that word which is settled; I decree, be settled, by that voice which establishes the earth may we be established; and by that command which all created things obey, may we be made the servants of the Lord God Almighty

PROPHETIC ORDINANCE

This is a physical expression of divine instructions under heaven to bring about divine manifestation of God's power on the earth and in human affairs. It is a prophetic act, aimed at stirring the supernatural.

Every sacrifice carried out in faith is an ordinance and whenever there is an ordinance, it stirred the supernatural up to act on behalf of the person or people behind the ordinance.

In the book of Exodus, God instructed the children of Israel to use the blood of an animal on their doorpost, because the angel of death was going to pass through every house in Egypt and any house without the blood on their doorpost the first born was going to die.

And if the household be too little for the lamb, let him and his neighbour next unto his house take it according to the number of the souls; every man according to his eating shall make your count for the lamb.
Your lamb shall be without blemish, a male of the first year: ye shall take it out from the sheep, or from the goats:
And ye shall keep it up until the fourteenth day of the same month: and the whole assembly of the congregation of Israel shall kill it in the evening.
And they shall take of the blood, and strike it on the two side posts and on the upper door post of the houses, wherein they shall eat it.
And they shall eat the flesh in that night, roast with fire, and unleavened bread; and with bitter herbs they shall eat it.
Eat not of it raw, nor sodden at all with water, but roast with fire; his head with his legs, and with the purtenance thereof.
And ye shall let nothing of it remain until the morning; and that which remaineth of it until the morning ye shall burn with fire.
And thus shall ye eat it; with your loins girded, your shoes on your feet, and your staff in your hand; and ye shall eat it in haste: it is the LORD's passover.
For I will pass through the land of Egypt this night, and will smite all the firstborn in the land of Egypt, both man and beast; and against all the gods of Egypt I will execute judgment: I am the LORD. Exodus 12:4-12.

Another graphic example of a divine ordinance is the story of the children of Israel walking around the wall of Jericho under a divine mandate.

Now Jericho was straitly shut up because of the children of Israel: none went out, and none came in.
And the LORD said unto Joshua, See, I have given into thine hand Jericho, and the king thereof, and the mighty men of valour.
And ye shall compass the city, all ye men of war, and go round

about the city once. Thus shalt thou do six days.
And seven priests shall bear before the ark seven trumpets of rams' horns: and the seventh day ye shall compass the city seven times, and the priests shall blow with the trumpets.
And it shall come to pass, that when they make a long blast with the ram's horn, and when ye hear the sound of the trumpet, all the people shall shout with a great shout; and the wall of the city shall fall down flat, and the people shall ascend up every man straight before him. Josh 6:1-5.

When the children of Israel obeyed and did as instructed, the wall came down and the children possessed the city.
The story of the priest bearing the Ark of the Covenant before the river Jordan is another illustration of an ordinance

The sea saw it and fled: Jordan was driven back. Psalm 114:3

In the book of Joshua:

And the LORD said unto Joshua, This day will I begin to magnify thee in the sight of all Israel, that they may know that, as I was with Moses, so I will be with thee.
And thou shalt command the priests that bear the ark of the covenant, saying, When ye are come to the brink of the water of Jordan, ye shall stand still in Jordan.
And Joshua said unto the children of Israel, Come hither, and hear the words of the LORD your God.
And Joshua said, Hereby ye shall know that the living God is among you and that he will without fail drive out from before you the Canaanites, and the Hittites, and the Hivites, and the Perizzites, and the Girgashites, and the Amorites, and the Jebusites.
Behold, the ark of the covenant of the Lord of all the earth passeth over before you into Jordan.
Now, therefore, take you twelve men out of the tribes of Israel, out of every tribe a man.
And it shall come to pass, as soon as the soles of the feet of the

priests that bear the ark of the LORD, the Lord of all the earth, shall rest in the waters of Jordan, that the waters of Jordan shall be cut off from the waters that come down from above; and they shall stand upon an heap. Josh 3:6-13.

In the New Testament, Jesus spat on the ground and use the clay to anoint the eyes of a blind man and gave an instruction on what should be done. Obedience to this instruction brought the visible manifestation of the perfected work in the spirit realm.

And as Jesus passed by, he saw a man which was blind from his birth.
And his disciples asked him, saying, Master, who did sin, this man, or his parents, that he was born blind?
Jesus answered, Neither hath this man sinned, nor his parents: but that the works of God should be made manifest in him.
I must work the works of him that sent me, while it is day: the night cometh, when no man can work.
As long as I am in the world, I am the light of the world.
When he had thus spoken, he spat on the ground, and made clay of the spittle, and he anointed the eyes of the blind man with the clay,
And said unto him, Go, wash in the pool of Siloam, (which is by interpretation, Sent.) He went his way therefore, and washed, and came seeing.
The neighbours therefore, and they which before had seen him that he was blind, said, Is not this he that sat and begged?
Some said, This is he: others said, He is like him: but he said, I am he.
Therefore said they unto him, How were thine eyes opened?
He answered and said, A man that is called Jesus made clay, and anointed mine eyes, and said unto me, Go to the pool of Siloam, and wash: and I went and washed, and I received sight. John 9:1-11.

CHAPTER 2

THE MYSTERY OF OIL

25 And thou shalt make it an oil of holy ointment, an ointment compound after the art of the apothecary: it shall be an holy anointing oil.
31 And thou shalt speak unto the children of Israel, saying, This shall be an holy anointing oil unto me throughout your generations. Exodus 30:25, 31.

There is something unique about the anointing oil. It's recorded in the Bible that when the anointing oil was poured on individuals, it set them apart for that specific purpose. They will see significant change around them and they embarked upon extraordinary exploits. The oil is a tool and agent of consecration. He who carries the oil carries the mandate and the oil release the power and presence of the Holy Spirit into such lives. Through this experience, the manifested power of deliverance, exaltation, promotion, favour and victory were poured into these individuals. This divine power is what God has destined for us to experience and put into action.
Naturally, oil makes an engine run smoothly, so it is in the spirit's realm. Oil greases the rough and tough road of destiny. The oil on you will put you ahead of your equal. The oil is an instrumentality of gladness wherever it shows up, sorrow turned into joy.

Thou lovest righteousness, and hatest wickedness: therefore God, thy God, hath anointed thee with the oil of gladness above thy fellows. Psalms 45:7.

And to them that are mourning the oil will turn their mourning into joy. The oil is an instrument of the enthronement of kings to the throne and priests to the office of priesthood.

The trees went forth on a time to anoint a king over them; and they said unto the olive tree, Reign thou over us.
But the olive tree said unto them, Should I leave my fatness, wherewith by me they honour God and man, and go to be promoted over the trees
Judges 9:8-9.

The oil indicates gladness, so its absence denoted sorrow or humiliation (Isa 61:3; Joel 2:19; Rev 6:6). It is on this principle that oil is so often used in the Scripture as a symbol of nourishment and comfort (Deut. 32:13; 33:24; Job 29:6; Psalm 45:7; 109:18; Isa 61:3).

OIL, which is the purest lighting material, has ever been a sacred symbol, possessing healing properties and ameliorating all suffering from wounds. Oil represents divine mercy in Christian symbolism. Thus, oil came to be used for anointing at baptism and confirmation, on the deathbed (the last anointing), at the ordination of priests, and the consecration of kings. The double sense of the performance was probably that it secures to the subject, first, a share of divine mercy, and, second, a strengthening for life's severe combats.

THE USE OF THE OIL IN THE OLD TESTAMENT

1. The consecration offering of priests (Exodus 29:2,23; Lev 6:15,21).
2. The offering of "beaten oil" with flour, which accompanied the daily sacrifice (Exodus29:40).
3. The leper's purification offering (Leviticus 14:10-18,21,24,28), where it is to be observed that the quantity of oil was invariable, while the other objects varied in quantity according to the means of the person offering. The cleansed leper was also to be touched with oil on various parts of his body (Leviticus 14:15-18).
4. The Nazarite, on completion of his vow, was to offer unleavened bread anointed with oil, and cakes of fine bread mingled with oil

(Number 6:15).
5. After the erection of the Tabernacle, the offerings of the "princes" included flour mingled with oil (Number 7).
6. At the consecration of the Levites, fine flour mingled with oil was offered (Number 8:8).
7. Meat offerings were mingled or anointed with oil (Leviticus 7:10,12).
On the other hand, certain offerings were to be devoid of oil: the sin-offering (Leviticus 5:11) and the offering of jealousy (Number 5:15).
8. Kings, priests, and prophets were anointed with oil or ointment.
7. As so important a necessary of life, the Jew was required to include oil among his first-fruit offerings (Ezekiel 22:29; 23:16; Number 18:12; Deuteronomy 18:4; 2 Chronicles 31:5).
b. Tithes of oil were also required (Deuteronomy. 12:17; 2 Chron 31:5; Neh 10:37,39; 13:12; Ezek 45:14).
8. Shields, if covered with hiding, were anointed with oil or grease previous to use. They perhaps rubbed over shields of metal in like manner to polish them.
9. Oil of inferior quality was used in the composition of soap.
10. Oil was poured on, or mixed with the flour or meal used in offerings.

The oil is a representation of the anointing, which is a burden destroyer and a yoke breaker. The oil brings easiness where there is friction.

And it shall come to pass in that day, that his burden shall be taken away from off thy shoulder, and his yoke from off thy neck, and the yoke shall be destroyed because of the anointing. Isaiah 10:27.

In the traditional circle, they used the oil for various things; they used it for the making of soap. It is an anti-poison agent and a balm for healing

And they cast out many devils, and anointed with oil many that

were sick, and healed them. Mark 6:13.

Is any among you afflicted? let him pray. Is any merry? let him sing psalms.
Is any sick among you? let him call for the elders of the church; and let them pray over him, anointing him with oil in the name of the Lord. James 5:13-14.

The oil is a tool of favour and exaltation. When the anointed oil comes upon a man, it set the man on the path of increase and exaltation.

But my horn shalt thou exalts like the horn of a unicorn: I shall be anointed with fresh oil. Psalm 92:10.

From the moment Prophet Samuel poured oil on Saul, the kingly anointing came on him, and exaltation and honour became his portion. The oil set Saul apart among his brethren.

Then Samuel took a vial of oil, and poured it upon his head, and kissed him, and said, Is it not because the LORD hath anointed thee to be captain over his inheritance?
When thou art departed from me to day, then thou shalt find two men by Rachel's sepulchre in the border of Benjamin at Zelzah; and they will say unto thee, The asses which thou wentest to seek are found: and, lo, thy father hath left the care of the asses, and sorroweth for you, saying, What shall I do for my son?
Then shalt thou go on forward from thence, and thou shalt come to the plain of Tabor, and there shall meet thee three men going up to God to Bethel, one carrying three kids, and another carrying three loaves of bread, and another carrying a bottle of wine:
And they will salute thee, and give thee two loaves of bread; which thou shalt receive of their hands. 1 Samuel 10:1-4.

My prayer is that the same oil that set David apart for a lifting will equally come upon you and set you apart for greatness in Jesus' name.

CHAPTER 3

THE MYSTERY OF THE SALT

The Salt is one of the prophetic tools, instruments and agents of savaging a situation that is already out of shape and where it is lacking, sweetness is lacking as well. It is a seasonal agent, and that is while Job said,

"Can that which is unsavoury be eaten without salt? Or is there any taste in the white of an egg?" Job 6:6.

Ye are the salt of the earth: but if the salt have lost his savour, wherewith shall it be salted? It is thenceforth good for nothing, but to be cast out, and to be trodden under foot of men. Matthew 5:13.

Salt is a preservative tool and an instrument for cleaning.

And as for thy nativity, in the day thou wast born thy navel was not cut, neither wast thou washed in water to supple thee; thou wast not salted at all, nor swaddled at all. Ezekiel 16:4.

And he said, Bring me a new cruse, and put salt therein. And they brought it to him.
And he went forth unto the spring of the waters, and cast the salt in there, and said, Thus saith the LORD, I have healed these waters; there shall not be from thence any more death or barren land. 2 King 2:20-21

There is hardly any food that is being prepared and eaten by humanity that is without. God commanded those meat offerings seasoned with salt (Lev 2:13). To eat salt with one is to partake of his hospitality, to derive subsistence from him; and hence he who

did so was bound to look after his host's interests (Ezra 4:14, "We have maintenance from the king's palace;" "We are salted with the salt of the palace" "We eat the salt of the palace").
Under the old covenant, every sacrifice was to have salt. The salt of the sacrifice is called the salt of the covenant because in common life salt was the symbol of the covenant; treaties being concluded and rendered firm and inviolable, according to a well-known custom of the ancient Greeks which is still kept among the Arabs, by the parties to an alliance eating bread and salt together, as a sign of the treaty which they had made. As a covenant, this kind was called a "covenant of salt," equivalent to an indissoluble covenant (Number 18:19; 2 Chronicles 13:5), so here the salt added to it designated the sacrifice as the salt of the covenant of God, because of its imparting strength and purity to the sacrifice, by which Israel received strength and fortification in covenant fellowship with God

Salt is a compound formed when the ionizable hydrogen of an acid is replaced by metallic or ammonium ions. There are different kinds of salt, soluble and insoluble. From a functional point of view, we can separate two kinds of salt, that is edible salt and industrial salt and both are not used for the same purpose.
The focus of this teaches is on the common salt. Salt is a chemical substance that contains sodium and chloride ions as the basic building elements. The neutralization reaction of an acid and a base produces it to give this substance sodium chloride (NACL)

The word salt has a connotation of high esteem and honour in ancient and modern times. Examples include the Arab Avowal "There is salt between us". The scripture uses the word salt figuratively; the New Unger's Bible Dictionary quotes.
As one of the most essential articles of food, salt symbolized the hospitality of good men, as opposing the spiritual corruption of sinners (Matt 5:13); of grace in the heart (Mark 9:50); of wisdom and good sense in speech (Col. 4:6); graceless believers as salt without savor (Matt 5:13; Mark 5:50) from the belief that salt

would, by exposure to the air, lose its virtue; salt pit was a figure of desolation (Zeph. 2:9); "salted with fire" (Mark 9:49) refers to the purification of the good and punishment of sinners.

Salt is one of the most important substances in human and animal diets. Most authorities consider common salt as an essential ingredient in our food. Most people intentionally season their cooking with more or less salt for the sake of palatability. Others depend upon the small quantities, which naturally exist in water and many foods, to furnish the amount of salt for the body. The ancient appreciated the value of salt for seasoning food (Job 6:6). Salt is so necessary that they dignified it by making it a requisite part of sacrifices (Leviticus 2:13; Ezra 2:9; Ezekiel 43:24; Mark 9:49).

The Secret of the Salt Covenant

There is an ancient Hebrew Leviticus covenant that, though only mentioned three times in the Bible, may hold the key to a great awakening in our nation. The Salt Covenant, a seemingly "minor" divine connection that's explicitly referenced in Leviticus 2:13 and Numbers 18:19, is actually alluded to throughout both the Old and New Testaments.

In 2 Chronicles 13:5, we see the power of this ancient covenant in action. Abijah, the king of Judah, stands with his 400,000 men ready for war against Israel's 800,000-soldier army, led by King Jeroboam. Most leaders in Abijah's position would think again before fighting an army twice its size, yet he seizes the opportunity to warn Israel that it should reconsider attacking because of a divine covenant Judah has based on... salt.

Ought ye not to know that the LORD God of Israel gave the kingdom over Israel to David for ever, even to him and to his sons by a covenant of salt? 2Chronicles13:5

Israel didn't heed the warning, and as a result, 500,000 of Jeroboam's men died—the largest single-day slaughter in history to this day.

Consider what an army of New Testament, Spirit-filled believers walking in the power of this Salt Covenant, could do today! We are in the mother of all spiritual battles, with our nation morally imploding before our eyes. Just as Israel sinned and forsook God, the nations of our world have rejected warning after warning. We must move into intense covenant power with God. This is the time for all believers to grasp the revelation of the Salt Covenant and walk in it.

What does salt look like? Throughout Scripture we find salt to be a true type of personal holiness. Jesus told us to "have salt in yourselves" (Mark 9:50). There has never been a genuine move of God that did not include the salt of personal holiness, nor will there ever be. Walking in holiness is key to experiencing the power of God in our lives. However, the Salt Covenant doesn't just include salt; there must be a sacrifice for the salt to go on. And here is where Leviticus 2:13 establishes a powerful biblical truth: Every sacrifice must have salt on it. This is why Jesus called Himself the "bread of life" (John 6:35), going beyond what the "grain offering" mentioned in Leviticus 2:13 could ever do. He is the one and only sacrifice for sin.

The Salt Covenant joins the imputed righteousness of God with the personal righteousness that every recipient of grace has the privilege and duty to walk in. Through Christ we can walk in this divine covenant and truly be, as He called us, the "salt of the earth" (Matt. 5:13) in a time when the church must once again walk in covenant with God if it hopes to continue to flourish.

Salt is an emblematic of loyalty and friendship. In the old testament times, a person who had undergone or joined in a 'salt covenant' with and then broke it was only fit to be cast out. Salt is used to ratify and seal covenant with God. The priest offered salt along with sacrifices whenever they appeared before God on behalf of the people.

A "Covenant of Salt"

All the heave offerings of the holy things, which the children of Israel offer unto the LORD, have I given thee, and thy sons and thy daughters with thee, by a statute forever: it is a covenant of salt for ever before the LORD unto thee and to thy seed with thee. Numbers 18:19;

Ought ye not to know that the LORD God of Israel gave the kingdom over Israel to David forever, even to him and to his sons by a covenant of salt? 2 Chronicles 13:5.

Covenant of salt is a covenant of perpetual obligation. New-born children were rubbed with salt;

And as for thy nativity, in the day thou wast born thy navel was not cut, neither wast thou washed in water to supple thee; thou wast not salted at all, nor swaddled at all. Ezekiel 16:4.

Disciples are likened unto salt, with reference to its cleansing and preserving uses.

Ye are the salt of the earth: but if the salt have lost his savour, wherewith shall it be salted? it is thenceforth good for nothing, but to be cast out, and to be trodden under foot of men. Matthew 5:13.

When Abimelech took the city of Shechem, he sowed the place with salt that it might always remain a barren soil. And Abimelech fought against the city all that day; and he took the city, and slew the people that was therein, and beat down the city, and sowed it with salt. Judges 9:45.

As salt was regarded as a necessary ingredient of the daily food, and so of all sacrifices offered to Yahweh (Lev 2:13), it became an easy step to the very close connection between salt and covenant-making. When men ate together they became friends. Consider the Arabic expression, "There is salt between us"; "He has eaten of my salt," which means partaking of hospitality which cemented friendship; compare "eat the salt of the palace" (Ezra 4:14). Covenants were generally confirmed by sacrificial meals and salt was always present. Since, too, salt is a preservative, it would

easily become symbolic of an enduring covenant. So offerings to Yahweh were to be by a statute forever, "a covenant of salt for ever before God" (Nu 18:19). David received his kingdom forever from God by a "covenant of salt" (2 Chronicles 13:5). In the light of these conceptions the remark of our Lord becomes the more significant: "Have salt in yourselves, and be at peace one with another"
Salt is good: but if the salt have lost his saltiness, wherewith will ye season it? Have salt in yourselves, and have peace one with another Mark 9:50.

Prophetic praying using salt is an eye opener to the mystery that has been hidden from so many people for centuries. It is an indispensable knowledge that every believing child of God must understand. It is a treasure that guarantees your victory over the satanic forces with which we contend, which diversify and sophisticate their modus operandi progressively. And because the knowledge from this would help you disarm the artillery of the devil.
To have salt in you is to have the fire of God in you because every believer is salted with fire.

For every one shall be salted with fire, and every sacrifice shall be salted with salt. Mark 9:49.

Salt is an ordinance of peace and favour and to lack salt is to lack the peace and favour of God.
Salt is good: but if the salt have lost his saltness, wherewith will ye season it? Have salt in yourselves, and have peace one with another. Mark 9:50
In every sacrifice, salt and fire was applied. So we see that wherever salt is there will also be fire! Salt and fire are partners in the process of PURIFICATION whereby 'the salt of the earth' will be purified, cleansed and preserved! The fire will burn up the dregs of salt that has lost its savour and leave us 'pure in heart'.
Perhaps you have felt that you have lost some of your earlier vitality and as the salt of the earth, not too salty or effective! Our God is MERCY- FULL and will replenish each salt supply. If we do

not request such a refreshing, we could easily get trodden under foot by circumstances of day-to-day living. We are told to have salt in ourselves and to have peace with one another. As the salt of the earth, we have been brought to the place of sacrifice by fire where our own ways and thinking must be cast out so that each one of us can be replenished with effective salt.

Such 'salt' will most certainly affect our relationships with other parts of the Body of Christ.

We must have salt in ourselves to move into that higher dimension that He has for us. We have to see it working out in us now, by having peace one with another. We cannot be upset, or 'uppity'! We must learn what the peace of God is. We need to see and know God truly pulling our hearts. Then we begin to realize that we are becoming that peace, and then we shall truly become peace makers. When the kingdom is functioning in us in fullness, we will be peace, and therefore fit to be a peacemaker. It is a progressive change.

USES OF SALT

1. Salt is used for preserving and seasoning (Matt 5:14). ye are the salt of the earth- what good is a salt that has lost flavour?

The Bible says salt and flavour is in us for preservation and seasoning... it brings sweetness to the substance; it also means salt can lose it flavour

2. Salt was used to ratify agreement so it became a symbol of faithfulness, as a symbol of faithfulness (Numbers 18:19) A covenant meal

2 A tool for sealing everlasting covenant, it indicates peace when salt is used to seal agreement. (chronic 13:5).

3. To purify and make whole, it is an emblem of quality of loyalty, no betrayal, faithful and accurate in friendship amongst Eastern nations

4. God required that every sacrificial meal should contain salt and it is also used as a faithfulness or covenant. e.g., covenant of peace. (Leviticus 2:13)

(Colossians 4:6), let your speech be always with grace, seasoned

with salt.
Have salt in yourself & have peace with one another. (mark 9:50)
Finally in prophetic warfare salt has two languages:
a) Purification - 2kings 2:19-21
b) Desolation (judges 9:45) However salt also has negative side but the focus here is on it uses. Repairing power, Cancellation of curses and it ability to deal with every form of bitterness

CHAPTER 4

THE MYSTERY OF THE SOAP AND WATER

And the earth was without form, and void, and darkness was upon the face of the deep. And the Spirit of God moved upon the face of the waters.
And God said, Let there be a firmament in the midst of the waters, and let it divide the waters from the waters.
And God said, Let the waters under the heaven be gathered together unto one place, and let the dry land appear: and it was so. Genesis 1:2, 6, 9.

Water is a substance composed of the chemical elements of hydrogen and oxygen and exists in gaseous, liquid, and solid states. Water is one of the most plentiful and essential compounds. It is vital to life, taking part in virtually every process that occurs in plants and animals. Although the molecules of water are simple in structure (H2O), the physical and chemical properties of the compound are extraordinarily complicated. See also ice; steam; water resources; precipitation.
Water is a colourless, tasteless, and odourless liquid at room temperature. One of its most important properties is its ability to dissolve many other substances. The versatility of water as a solvent is essential for living organisms to function with ease. Many people believed that life originated in the world's oceans, which are complicated solutions. Living organisms use aqueous solutions—e.g., blood and digestive juices—as mediums for carrying out biological processes.
The Earth is a watery place. But just how much water exists on, in, and above our planet? About 71 percent of the Earth's surface

is water-covered, and the oceans hold about 96.5 percent of all Earth's water. Water also exists in the air as water vapour, in rivers and lakes, in icecaps and glaciers, in the ground as soil moisture and in aquifers, and even in you and your dog.

Water is never sitting still. Thanks to the water cycle, our planet's water supply is constantly moving from one place to another and from one form to another. Things would get pretty stale without the water cycle!

Water is indeed essential for all life on, in, and above the Earth. This is important to you because you are made up mostly of water. Water is of major importance to all living things; in some organisms, up to 90% of their body weight comes from water. Up to 60% of the human adult body is water.

According to H.H. Mitchell, the brain and heart are composed of 73% water, and the lungs are about 83% water. The skin contains 64% water, muscles and kidneys are 79%, and even the bones are watery: 31%.

Each day humans must consume a certain amount of water to survive. Of course, this varies according to age and gender, and also by where someone lives. An adult male needs about 3 liters (3.2 quarts) per day while an adult female needs about 2.2 liters (2.3 quarts) per day. All the water a person need does not have to come from drinking liquids, as some of this water is contained in the food we eat.

Water serves several essential functions to keep us all going

A vital nutrient to the life of every cell acts first as a building material.

It regulates our internal body temperature by sweating and respiration

Water metabolizes and transports the carbohydrates and proteins that our bodies use as food in the bloodstream; It helps flush waste mainly through urination and acts as a shock absorber for the brain, spinal cord, and fetus forms. Saliva lubricates water metabolizes and transports joints our bodies use as food in the bloodstream. No less important is the ability of water to transport waste material out of our bodies.

When we read through the scripture, we see after the creation of heaven and the earth; water covered the earth. We see how God moved upon the water to bring salvation and deliverance to his people. When God wanted to wipe away humanity in the days of Noah, He deployed the instrument of water to fill the earth.

4 For yet seven days, and I will cause it to rain upon the earth forty days and forty nights, and every living substance that I have made will I destroy from off the face of the earth.
17 And the flood was forty days upon the earth, and the waters increased, and bare up the ark, and it was lifted above the earth.
18 And the waters prevailed and were increased greatly upon the earth, and the ark went upon the face of the waters.
19 And the waters prevailed exceedingly upon the earth; and all the high hills that were under the whole heaven were covered.
23 And every living substance was destroyed which was upon the face of the ground, both man, and cattle, and the creeping things, and the fowl of the heaven; and they were destroyed from the earth: and Noah only remained alive, and they that were with him in the ark. Gen 7:4, 17-19,23.

Water can either be an incredible blessing or an all-destroying curse. In some instances, the water of God is a picture of the Holy Spirit of God that is the water of life, bringing refreshment as pleasant as a clear, cool, bubbling spring in a hot and dusty desert. On other occasions, water is used as a barrier or test of consecration that one has to "pass through" to crossover into God's blessing, e.g. crossing the Red Sea or Jordan River and Baptism. The Water of God is a purifier.

Water is essential to life, which is why people mostly live, where water is easily available, and rain comes with abundant regularity. Especially for those who live in marginal regions, water is critical and must be pumped from the underground or piped from another region.

Otherwise, the area is left uninhabited, because there is no life

without water.
The foundation of the whole earth and the entire world is water

The earth is the LORD's, and the fulness thereof; the world, and they that dwell therein.
For he hath founded it upon the seas, and established it upon the floods. Psalm 24:1-2.

The voice of the Lord is upon the waters; the God of glory thunders; the Lord is upon many waters.
The Lord sat as King over the deluge; the Lord still sits as King and forever. Psalm 29: 3, 10:
And in front of the throne, there was also what looked like a transparent glassy sea, as if of Crystal. Rev. 4:6.

Here, Apostle John is talking about the sea. There is more than the eyes can see in the water body (sea), there are more creatures
The water and soap are agents of cleaning. When a surface is dirty and soap and water is applied a cleaning takes place.
Water is a powerful instrument. Over half of the earth's surface is covered with was and the human body is about seventy water. At creation, after God created heaven and the earth, the earth was completely covered with water.
Just as water is an instrument,

For though thou wash thee with nitre, and take thee much soap, yet thine iniquity is marked before me, saith the Lord GOD. Jeremiah 2:22.

But who may abide the day of his coming? and who shall stand when he appeareth? for he is like a refiner's fire, and like fullers' soap: Malachi 3:2.

When the instrument of water and soap are tools of a prophetic ordinance, they act not only as an instrument of cleaning but all human, despite their colour and race uses them, that is why when you visit most water; you find a lot of human activities, and sacrifices made there. The water and soap ordinance is a deliverance tool.

CHAPTER 5

THE MYSTERY OF THE HONEY

HONEY. A sweet, liquid substance produced by bees or, artificially, from fruit. The Old Testament often refers to honey, using a Hebrew word that, when translated, means "sweet substance" since it's a material that comes from sources other than bees.

Pleasant words are as an honeycomb, sweet to the soul, and health to the bones. Proverb 16:24.

But Jonathan heard not when his father charged the people with the oath: wherefore he put forth the end of the rod that was in his hand, and dipped it in an honeycomb, and put his hand to his mouth, and his eyes were enlightened. 1 Samuel 14:27.

The story of Samson's riddle (Judg 14) is one passage where the Hebrew word must certainly refer to honey. Bees and honey are mentioned together in this text. It is also possible to interpret the honey in the story of Jonathan and Saul's vow (1 Sam 14) as the product of bees.

The word honey can also refer to a thick syrup made from grapes and dates. In Arabic, the word used for this kind of fruit syrup is the same as the Hebrew word for honey from bees.

Typically, honey is composed of natural sugars and minerals. It contains phosphates, calcium, iron, magnesium potassium and sodium chloride. The percentages vary among the different varietals of honey. Some honey varieties have additional compounds, depending on what they were made of. On average,

honey contains 80% natural sugars in the following forms:
Glucose: 31.3%
Fructose: 38.2%
Maltose: 7.1%
Sucrose: 1.3%
Higher sugars: 1.5%
Honey has high fructose content, besides the other forms of sugar. Therefore, honey is sweeter than refined sugars and other sweeteners. It also has higher calorie content.
Other components include:
Ash: 0.2%
Water: 17.2%
Other/undetermined: 3.2%
Pollen, protein, minerals and vitamins: 2%
Water content is desirable at less than 18%. Honey has better quality if there is less water in it.
Vitamins and other nutrient contents are mainly based on where the nectar came from. On average, honey contains riboflavin, niacin, thiamin, vitamin B6 and pantothenic acid. It also contains some amino acids. Mineral content includes iron, copper, calcium, phosphorus, manganese, magnesium, sodium, zinc and potassium. A few experts measure the mineral content through the conductivity of the honey. Higher conductivities mean higher mineral contents. Manuka honey, for example, contains 4 times more minerals than most kinds of honey because it is 4 times higher than the average honey in terms of conductivity.
As a symbol, honey stands for abundance (Ex 3:8; 13:5; 33:3), the believer's delight in God's word (Ps 19:10; 119:103), and the rightness of God's word to His people (Ezek 3:3).
In Old Testament times, as at present, honey was rare enough to be considered a luxury (Gen 43:11; 1 Kings 14:3). We used honey in baking sweets (Ex 16:31). It was forbidden to be offered with the meal-offering (Lev 2:11), perhaps because it was fermentable, but was presented with the fruit offering (2 Chron 31:5). Honey was offered to David's army (2 Sam 17:29). It was sometimes stored in the fields (Jer 41:8). It was also exchanged as

merchandise (Ezek 27:17). In New Testament times, wild honey was an article of food among the lowly (Matt 3:4; Mark 1:6).
Honey, one of the oldest sweeteners, comes from flower nectar that has been consumed by the honey bee
Honey: a sweet viscid material elaborated out of the nectar of flowers in the honey sac of various bees.

HOW HONEY IS MADE

Honey is made by bees in their hives. The process starts with the collection of nectars from flowers by the worker bees. The collected nectars are placed in honeycombs. The bees fan it with their wings to evaporate most of the water in the nectar. They also add enzymes to aid in honey production. In the process, the natural sugars in the nectar are also broken down into simple forms.
As the water evaporates, the remaining liquid turns thicker, and the sugar becomes concentrated, turning it into a thick and sweet liquid. When about 17% of the water content is removed, the bees seal the cells of the honeycomb with beeswax. Over time, chemical reactions and more evaporation take place, turning the liquid into honey.
The colour and flavour of the honey largely depend on the type of flower where the nectar came from. Honey blends occur naturally, as the bees collect honey from all kinds of flowers. This happens often when the beehive is close to an area with different flowers growing nearby. When the number of bees is few to collect nectar from particular flowers, they fetched specific flavours
For example, the beehive is in the middle of a field of sunflowers, there is no other kind of flower nearby. The bees would produce sunflower honey, pure and unblended.

NATURAL BENEFITS OF HONEY

Honey has a long history of being used for its medicinal properties. Ancient civilizations, such as the Greeks and the Egyptians, had been using honey to treat various ailments and to improve health. They found one Egyptian tomb containing a thousand-year-old jar containing honey.

The natural and healthy sweetness of honey also makes it a good, healthy sweetener. It contained nutrients that help heal and preserve health.

THE FOLLOWING ARE SOME OF THE HEALTH BENEFITS OBTAINED FROM HONEY:

1. Lower your risk of heart disease.
2. Enhance your immune system.
3. Stave off diabetes.
4. Treat respiratory diseases.
5. Heal wounds.
6. Slow the ageing process.
7. Add years to your life.
8. Enhances calcium absorption
9. Speeds up healing of stomach ulcers
10. Acts as a natural, yet gentle laxative
11. Controls insulin and blood sugar levels
12. Helps treat anaemia
13. Prevents low white blood cell levels
14. Relieve allergy symptoms
15. Treats allergies
16. Helps with alcohol metabolism
17. Good workout energy source
18. Helps treat dandruff and scalp problems
19. Treats common cold

UNBELIEVABLE HEALING HINTS OF HONEY

1. Honey varietals come from different shrubs, trees, flowers, and other plants—offering you different flavours and aromas.
2. Poly-floral honey is made from over one type of flower; mono-floral is made from one specific type—like single-origin, dark chocolate.
3. The darker the honey, the more antioxidants and the stronger the flavour.
4. Honey offers different healing powers. Manuka and sidr stick

out on the list of standout kinds of honey.

5. Honey, dark, light, or antioxidant richer than others, gets better when infused with nature's herbs, spices, and fruits. Not only do these ingredients boost flavour and texture—but they can also add more vitamins, minerals, and antioxidants.

6. Flavored/fruited honey and Mix-In kinds of honey give you more flavour and healthful herbs, peels, and spices.

7. Artisanal honey sauces and dressings paired with olive oil, vinegar, and chocolate offer extra healing powers.

HONEY AS A PROPHETIC ORDINANCE

Honey is a prophetic tool used for prophetic prayers. The honey is a prophetic ordinance used in prayer to turn bitter water into a sweet one and an ugly experience into a glorious one. Honey has been in use for over decades in wedding ceremonies and naming ceremonies because of the belief that it has the potential to attract blessings when used in prayer.

CHAPTER 6

THE MYSTERY OF THE PERFUME

And thou shalt make it a perfume, a confection after the art of the apothecary, tempered together, pure and holy:
And as for the perfume which thou shalt make, ye shall not make to yourselves according to the composition thereof: it shall be unto thee holy for the LORD. Exodus 30:35, 37.
Ointment and perfume rejoice the heart: so doth the sweetness of a man's friend by hearty counsel. Proverb 27:9.

Perfumes are a substance that emits a nice fragrant product that results from the artful blending of certain odoriferous substances in the right proportions. The word perfume is derived from the Latin word "per fumum," meaning "through the smoke." The ancients discovered and master the art of perfumery. We find references to perfumery materials and formulas in the Bible.
Using perfumes was common among the Hebrews and the Orientals before it became known to the Greeks and Romans. Moses also speaks of the art of the perfumer in the English Bible "apothecary;" and gives the composition of two perfumes, of which one was to be offered to the Lord on the golden altar,
And the LORD said unto Moses, Take unto thee sweet spices, stacte, and onycha, and galbanum; these sweet spices with pure frankincense: of each shall there be a like weight:
And thou shalt make it a perfume, a confection after the art of the apothecary, tempered together, pure and holy:
And thou shalt beat some of it very small, and put of it before the testimony in the tabernacle of the congregation, where I will meet with thee: it shall be unto you most holy.

And as for the perfume which thou shalt make, ye shall not make to yourselves according to the composition thereof: it shall be unto thee holy for the LORD.
Whosoever shall make like unto that, to smell thereto, shall even be cut off from his people. Exodus 30:34-38.

And the other to be used for anointing the high priest and his sons, the tabernacle, and the vessels of divine service, Exodus 30:23-33.

And he came near, and kissed him: and he smelled the smell of his raiment, and blessed him, and said, See, the smell of my son is as the smell of a field which the LORD hath blessed: Genesis27:27.

All of God's creation has an identity and odour that was while Isaac said, "See, the smell of my son is as the smell of a field which the LORD hath blessed". Every field has a smell and a smell will attract or repel. A field that God has blessed is a field that is well-favoured. The perfume causes a sensual delight and makes the heart rejoice.
Campbell Morgan was visiting the home of a friend. In one room, he always detected the fragrance of roses. One day he said to his friend, "I wish you would tell me how. I never come into this room without smelling roses." His friend smiled and said, "Ten years ago I was in the Holy Land where I bought a small vial of attar of roses. I wrapped it in cotton wool, and as I was standing here unpacking it, suddenly I broke the bottle. I took the whole thing, cotton wool and all, and put it into this vase." That fragrance had permeated the clay of the vase, and it was impossible to enter the room without consciousness of it. If Christ is in us, the fragrance of the Rose of Sharon will pervade and permeate our whole life. "Like a sweet smell that spreads everywhere, God uses us to make Christ known to all men." (2 Cor. 2:15) Good News for Modern Man.
A smell can be pleasant or unpleasant. In the spirit's realm, the odour is significant; that is why the devil is called a foul or unclean spirit. In the school of deliverance, we know that sometimes when

demons are cast out; you perceive a bad smell because demons have a foul odour.

When Jesus saw that the people came running together, he rebuked the foul spirit, saying unto him, Thou dumb and deaf spirit, I charge thee, come out of him, and enter no more into him. Mark 9:25.

And he cried mightily with a strong voice, saying, Babylon the great is fallen, is fallen, and is become the habitation of devils, and the hold of every foul spirit, and a cage of every unclean and hateful bird. Revelation 18:2.

Smells either repel or attract and every man carries a smell. It can either be pleasant or not is another matter entirely. The good & pleasant smell naturally endeared people to us. The patriarch Isaac understood this better when he likened the smell of his son to be as the smell of the field which the Lord has blessed, the field here can be likened to a well-watered garden that flourishes & brings good fruit that will not only be pleasing to the eyes but will taste well when eaten.

As believers, our fruits should be the fruit of the spirit.

And he cried mightily with a strong voice, saying, Babylon the great is fallen, is fallen, and is become the habitation of devils, and the hold of every foul spirit, and a cage of every unclean and hateful bird.

As a Christian, you are expected to exude the fruit of the spirit so our lives can smell like the field that the Lord has blessed.

It is these fruits that will bring out the kind of smell that Isaac was talking about.

The manifestation of these fruits of the Holy Spirit in Galatians 5:22-26: are love, joy, peace, long-suffering, gentleness, goodness, faith, meekness & temperance.

Coincidentally, there are 9 fruits synonymous with 9 months of pregnancy and eventually giving birth to a good character that exudes flavour that brings favour.

It is the character/fruit of an individual that first smells out before

you perceive their body smell. So, if your smell is unpleasant, check your relationship with God. Take out time to mend the field & see that the fruit will be good and pleasant.
There are some believers whose smell has brought disfavour and repelled their benefactors away. Some marriages have been destroyed because the husband or wife started emitting unpleasant smells. While some others carry a demonic aroma that dispels favour and if you are in that category, the Lord deliver you completely, in Jesus' name.
For others, it may be the way they talk (mouth odour or body odour) that repels their helpers and their manner of approach. Today, the blood of Jesus is ready to wash away every unpleasant smell and set you free in Jesus' name. Amen.

Mary then comes to Jesus with Martha's encouragement, falling at his feet when she does. "If you had been here, Lord, my brother would not have died," she says through her tears. She, a friend, also cannot see the bigger picture. The two of them are surrounded by mourners, and when he asks about Lazarus's body, these others speak Jesus' line - "Come and see!" However, theirs is an invitation to observe death, not life. This is too much, and Jesus weeps in frustration
(John11:28-37).
From there he goes to the tomb and, by his word, raises Lazarus from the dead (11:38-44) - a foretaste of what lies around the next bend in Jerusalem. The die is cast. His opponents now decide the time has come for this "one man to die than the whole nation not be destroyed" (11:45-57). Passover is near. And so we arrive at this text.
Overall, it is the fragrance of the oil, and also of Mary's deed, which is the pleasing aroma that is common to all four gospels. Mary's selfless act of devotion and adoration of him, who is the resurrection and the life, invites us to remember what she did.
She put into her hands what she couldn't speak from her lips. And, her action took on a new meaning after she did it. Though probably not conscious of the fact that Mary was preparing Jesus'

body for death. They didn't leave that up to the funeral director back in those days. The family took the deceased and lovingly washed the body one last time, using fragrant oil, and then wrapped it in a shroud. There wasn't time on Friday when Jesus died for them to properly prepare his body. Sabbath was coming at sunset, and you do not even do that kind of work on the day of rest.

It was on the third day of death, when the women came with their water and aromatic oil to finish the job, that something new was discovered. Like at Bethany, the stone had been rolled away, and the tomb was empty. Mary had, indeed, earlier been the one who last anointed Jesus and prepared him for death. The fragrance of that oil could still be smelled. Only now, it was like the aroma of an offering to God. For that is what Jesus had done upon the cross. He gave his life as an offering, a sacrifice for us. Ephesians 5:2.

Do you smell it? The aroma of his love fills this room, even today! The fragrance of it is filling the world...

As we walk through the Garden of life in Christ's Jesus, it is my hope and prayer that we will pick up some of the holy fragrance of God's love for us. And as we go back into our daily activities and display our sweet fragrance of Christ's love.

As Mary poured out her perfume on Jesus' feet as an act of adoration and total devotion in preparation for his death, let us also pour out our lives as a holy and fragrant offering to Christ.

When Jesus gave himself up for us, dying upon the cross, this expression of love was "a fragrant offering and sacrifice to God." (Ephesians 5:2b) The aroma of it still lingers in this world. We could say that the "scent" of his love has attracted and made us what we are today. As I conclude this chapter, I say, be filled with the holy fragrance of God's love for sinful mankind, may God's pleasing aroma cling to our lives. Others will know us by this love. As followers of Jesus Christ we are in the business of providing "aromatherapy" - that is, sharing the "pleasant odour" of his love in a world that all too often stinks.

CHAPTER 7

THE MYSTERY OF THE SAND

And the LORD God formed man of the dust of the ground, and breathed into his nostrils the breath of life, and man became a living soul. Genesis 2:7

And the LORD God formed man of the dust of the ground, and breathed into his nostrils the breath of life, and man became a living soul. Genesis 2:7 (NETB)

The Lord God took a handful of soil and made a man. God breathed life into the man, and the man started breathing. Genesis 2:7 (CEV)

The human body that carries the spirit of God is a container made of sand that is why God said "Then shall the dust return to the earth as it was: and the spirit shall return unto God who gave it". Ecclesiastes12:7.

Every affair of human living is carried out on the ground and therefore sand plays a significant role in all human activities, sand is valuable and its value varies from coast to coast, all that man lives by comes out of the ground, and there is something about the sand more than the human eyes can see.

All of the major activities of creation take place on the earth, every human being stands on the earth, it does not matter whether you are high or low, all humans, fly, you will still land on the earth, swim in an endless ocean you will come to a landing place on the earth. The sand is a weapon of war; the scripture gives us an insight into when the Lord told Moses to use the dust (sand).

And the LORD said unto Moses, say unto Aaron, Stretch out thy rod, and smite the dust of the land, that it may become lice throughout all the land of Egypt.
And they did so; for Aaron stretched out his hand with his rod, and smote the dust of the earth, and it became lice in man, and in beast; all the dust of the land became lice throughout all the land of Egypt.
And the magicians did so with their enchantments to bring forth lice, but they could not: so there were lice upon man, and upon beast.
Then the magicians said unto Pharaoh, This is the finger of God: and Pharaoh's heart was hardened, and he hearkened not unto them; as the LORD had said. Exodus 8: 16-19.

The prophet praying in the book of Jeremiah 22:29-30 said:

O earth, earth, earth, hear the word of the LORD.
Thus saith the LORD, Write ye this man childless, a man that shall not prosper in his days: for no man of his seed shall prosper, sitting upon the throne of David, and ruling any more in Judah.

You need to have an understanding of the mystery of the sand and how to appropriate it as a weapon of war, favour and instrument of help. When the earth writes one childless, he or she will remain childless unless his feet do not touch the earth and when the rises up in your aid, friends, you are helped.

When Korah and his company gather against Moses, the servant of God prayed and the earth reacted against those that revolted against him.

And Moses said unto Korah, Be thou and all thy company before the LORD, thou, and they, and Aaron, to morrow:
And take every man his censer, and put incense in them, and bring ye before the LORD every man his censer, two hundred and

**fifty censers; thou also, and Aaron, each of you his censer.
And they took every man his censer, and put fire in them, and laid incense thereon, and stood in the door of the tabernacle of the congregation with Moses and Aaron.
And Korah gathered all the congregation against them unto the door of the tabernacle of the congregation: and the glory of the LORD appeared unto all the congregation.
And the LORD spake unto Moses and unto Aaron, saying,
Separate yourselves from among this congregation, that I may consume them in a moment.
And they fell upon their faces, and said, O God, the God of the spirits of all flesh, shall one man sin, and wilt thou be wroth with all the congregation?
And the LORD spake unto Moses, saying,
Speak unto the congregation, saying, Get you up from about the tabernacle of Korah, Dathan, and Abiram.
And Moses rose up and went unto Dathan and Abiram, and the elders of Israel followed him.
And he spake unto the congregation, saying, Depart, I pray you, from the tents of these wicked men, and touch nothing of theirs, lest ye be consumed in all their sins.
So they gat up from the tabernacle of Korah, Dathan, and Abiram, on every side: and Dathan and Abiram came out, and stood in the door of their tents, and their wives, and their sons, and their little children.
And Moses said, Hereby ye shall know that the LORD hath sent me to do all these works; for I have not done them of mine own mind.
If these men die the common death of all men, or if they be visited after the visitation of all men; then the LORD hath not sent me. {the common...: Heb. as every man dieth}
But if the LORD make a new thing, and the earth open her mouth, and swallow them up, with all that appertain unto them, and they go down quick into the pit; then ye shall understand that these men have provoked the LORD. {make...: Heb. create a creature}**

And it came to pass, as he had made an end of speaking all these words, that the ground clave asunder that was under them:
And the earth opened her mouth, and swallowed them up, and their houses, and all the men that appertained unto Korah, and all their goods. Number 16:16-32.

In the book of Revelation the woman with a child that the dragon was against, it was the earth that helped her.

And when the dragon saw that he was cast unto the earth, he persecuted the woman which brought forth the man child.
And to the woman were given two wings of a great eagle, that she might fly into the wilderness, into her place, where she is nourished for a time, and times, and half a time, from the face of the serpent.
And the serpent cast out of his mouth water as a flood after the woman, that he might cause her to be carried away of the flood.
And the earth helped the woman, and the earth opened her mouth, and swallowed up the flood which the dragon cast out of his mouth.
And the dragon was wroth with the woman, and went to make war with the remnant of her seed, which keep the commandments of God, and have the testimony of Jesus Christ. Revelation 12:13-17

The earth can refuse to give a man increase when it becomes brass and as result, as long as you walk on the earth when it becomes brass, nothing works

And I will break the pride of your power; and I will make your heaven as iron, and your earth as brass: Leviticus 26:19.

When the earth becomes brass, you get dust in the place of the yield of the field, Isaac was praying for his son

Therefore God give thee of the dew of heaven, and the fatness of the earth, and plenty of corn and wine: Genesis 27:28.

A man's ground can be blessed or cursed, when someone's ground is under a curse, nothing that is planted there will yield an increase but when someone's ground is blessed whatever one sow yields bountifully. God said to Adam thy ground is cursed

And unto Adam he said, Because thou hast hearkened unto the voice of thy wife, and hast eaten of the tree, of which I commanded thee, saying, Thou shalt not eat of it: cursed is the ground for thy sake; in sorrow shalt thou eat of it all the days of thy life;
In the sweat of thy face shalt thou eat bread, till thou return unto the ground; for out of it wast thou taken: for dust thou art, and unto dust shalt thou return. Genesis 3:17, 19.

Till today man has not total recovery from that curse, man will have to sweat out everything to earn a living. My prayer is that your ground will be blessed and your earth will yield an increase in Jesus' name. Amen.

And he looked this way and that way, and when he saw that there was no man, he slew the Egyptian and hid him in the sand. Exodus 2:12.

The symbol of the sand is very important. The meaning of the sand according to Genesis chapter 2 forms the basis of our existence in life. The human being came out from the body of the dust.
And the Lord God formed man of the dust of the ground, and breathed into his nostrils the breath of life; and man became a living soul. Genesis 2:7.

The connection between God and man and man to dust sparked off the power of God Almighty. Sand or dust has a hidden power. The power of God charged the dust or sand to form man. Dust or sand has a resurrecting and binding power. Whenever there is a heavy blowing of the wind, it will surely carry the particle of the dust. The foundation of the sand which the Bible described as the dust has made so many people wonder why God uses the dust to create human beings. This is one part of God that no one has yet to fully understand the mystery of the Almighty God.

Then shall the dust return to the earth as it was: and the spirit shall return unto God who gave it. Ecclesiastes 12:7

It is a common practice to see some people sprinkle dust on the dead body. For example, if you have been to the burial ground or in a funeral ceremony, you will hear this word, "Dust thou art and unto the dust thou shall return. One of the reasons most religious bodies are practising this is because of the place of the above verse. Some evil people draw evil spirits from the sand and direct them against people. They can use the sand to command sorrow into the life of a person. Satanic power picks up the sand, speaks to it and blows it into the air to completely paralyze a person's destiny

Thou shalt not be afraid for the terror by night; nor for the arrow that flieth by day Psalm 91:5.

One of the most powerful weapons used by wicked people is sand or dust. Many people have been suffering from the power of dust or sand. When somebody is under attack by the arrow of the sand, the person will notice an embargo on his progress. People who use dust or sand are very terrible. When the arrow of sand or dust is working against a person, the person may suffer from marriage or business destruction. The multiple afflictions that people suffer especially when they are in a business relationship are caused by the arrow of the sand.

And the Lord said unto Moses and unto Aaron, Take to you handfuls of ashes of the furnace, and let Moses sprinkle it toward the heaven in the sight of Pharaoh. And it shall become small dust in all the land of Egypt, and shall be a boil breaking forth with blains upon man, and upon beast, throughout all the land of Egypt. And they took ashes of the furnace, and stood before Pharaoh; and Moses sprinkled it up toward heaven; and it became a boil breaking forth with blains upon man, and upon beast. And the magicians could not stand before Moses because of the boils; for the boil was upon the magicians, and upon all the

Egyptians. And the Lord hardened the heart of Pharaoh, and he hearkened not unto them; as the Lord had spoken unto Moses." Exodus 9: 8-12.

Some satanic agents can charm the ground, and if you do not have the fire of God and you pass the palace, you will be in trouble. Satan has learnt the secret of the sand and dust and has put it to work as a witchcraft attack. Satanic agents remove the dust or sand from the threshold of the person's house or place of business and speak poverty into it and the person cannot prosper

In Exodus 8:16-17
And the LORD said unto Moses, Say unto Aaron, Stretch out thy rod, and smite the dust of the land, that it may become lice throughout all the land of Egypt. And they did so; for Aaron stretched out his hand with his rod, and smote the dust of the earth, and it became lice in man, and in beast; all the dust of the land became lice throughout all the land of Egypt.

In other to fight the Egyptians, Moses had to smite the dust to release lice on the Egyptians. The dust can carry messages.

When a person is under the attack of the sand, the person may suddenly become insane. The enemies used sand to arrest the glory of so many people. If you do not know how to counter them, you will move from trouble to trouble. Many destinies are buried in the earth (SAND OR DUST). The dust or sand can carry positive or negative instructions. The earth which we stand upon carries the virtue of people. They can carry information about you very fast as long as you are still walking on the surface of the earth.
When the enemy sees somebody prospering more than them, they try to reverse the situation.
Through the dust, a believer can issue curses upon a land. Through the dust, Moses brought afflictions to the people of Egypt. A believer can speak to the dust and counter any attacks coming against them. So fighting with the dust is a spiritual law. The dark powers can network and coordinate their operation

effectively through the dust because we transfer dust from place to place.

CHAPTER 8

THE MYSTERY OF THE HOLY COMMUNION

One of the greatest mysteries of the Bible is the Holy Communion which is a New Testament mystery meant to give man mastery over all forms of weaknesses, sickness and all forms of demonic assault. This mystery was designed to actualize the flow of eternal life in our body causing us to walk in total wholeness in our everyday experiences.
Communion was first recorded in the Bible when Abram returned from rescuing his nephew Lot, Lot's family and his goods. Melchizedek served Abram bread and wine and blessed him. Then Abram gave Melchizedek tithes of all he had.

And Melchizedek king of Salem brought forth bread and wine: and he was the priest of the most high God.
And he blessed him, and said, Blessed be Abram of the most high God, possessor of heaven and earth:
And blessed be the most high God, which hath delivered thine enemies into thy hand. And he gave him tithes of all. Genesis 14:18-20.

The above Bible passage suggests a relationship between Communion (or Eucharist as it is called by many

Jesus spook concerning this mystery in the book of John.

This is the bread which cometh down from heaven, that a man may eat thereof, and not die.
I am the living bread which came down from heaven: if any man eat of this bread, he shall live forever: and the bread that I will give is my flesh, which I will give for the life of the world.

The Jews, therefore, strove among themselves, saying, How can this man give us his flesh to eat?
Then Jesus said unto them, Verily, verily, I say unto you, Except ye eat the flesh of the Son of man, and drink his blood, ye have no life in you.
Whoso eateth my flesh, and drinketh my blood, hath eternal life; and I will raise him up at the last day.
For my flesh is meat indeed, and my blood is drink indeed.
He that eateth my flesh, and drinketh my blood, dwelleth in me, and I in him.
As the living Father hath sent me, and I live by the Father: so he that eateth me, even he shall live by me.
This is that bread which came down from heaven: not as your fathers did eat manna, and are dead: he that eateth of this bread shall live forever. John 6:50-58.

This mystery is a total representation of all the finished work of Christ. You cannot understand the totality of all that Jesus did until the mystery of communion. The mystery is about the body and the blood of Jesus, anyone who eats of his body and blood shall not die.

In the old testament in the days of Elisha, there was a graphic illustration of a type and shadow of the mystery of the communion.
One of the sons of the prophets went out to gather herbs to add to their pottage for lunch. But after cooking and eating all the sons of the prophet were down. They cried out to Elisha "... there is death in the pot"

And Elisha came again to Gilgal: and there was a dearth in the land; and the sons of the prophets were sitting before him: and he said unto his servant, Set on the great pot, and seethe pottage for the sons of the prophets.
And one went out into the field to gather herbs, and found a wild vine, and gathered thereof wild gourds his lap full, and came and shred them into the pot of pottage: for they knew them not.

So they poured out for the men to eat. And it came to pass, as they were eating of the pottage, that they cried out, and said, O thou man of God, there is death in the pot. And they could not eat thereof.
But he said, Then bring meal. And he cast it into the pot; and he said, Pour out for the people, that they may eat. And there was no harm in the pot. 2King 4:38-41

"Death in the pot" connotes that the food was poisoned, Elisha responded "...bring the meal" and when he threw the meal in the pot, there was no more harm. What he threw in to swallow up all poison in the pot.

The Communion table is not a religious snack. It is one of the vital ministries of the New Testament.
"The Lord's Supper is a commemorative ordinance, a memorial of Christ's atoning sacrifice on the cross. It is a feast of the living union of believers with the Saviour, whereby they truly, that is spiritually and by faith, receive Christ with all His benefits, and are nourished with His life unto eternal life"
The ultimate of the Communion is for us to live like Jesus.
"The Supper is a personal fellowship with Christ. Partaking of one bread creates fellowship between the members too; it merges them into one body, the church"
In John 6:48-54 Jesus says I am the bread of life; if you eat of bread you will live forever. So the God kind of life is transmitted through the bread.
By taking communion we are deemed to live (divine life) like Jesus.

The ministry of the communion table ministers to your 3 Dimensional Being. Hebrew 9:14: 14 How much more, then, will the blood of Christ, who through the eternal Spirit offered himself unblemished to God, cleanse our consciences from acts that lead to death, so that we may serve the living God! The blood can purge my conscience from every evil work.
The Blood of Jesus is the only treatment of the conscience of a man.

Therefore, since we have these promises, dear friends, let us purify ourselves from everything that contaminates body and spirit, perfecting holiness out of reverence for God. The filthiness of the flesh and spirit is cleansed. 2 Corinthians 7:11

May God himself, the God of peace, sanctify you through and through. May your whole spirit, soul and body be kept blameless at the coming of our Lord Jesus Christ. May the whole of your being be sanctified. 1 Thessalonians 5:23.

When he was at the table with them, he took bread, gave thanks, broke it and began to give it to them.
Then their eyes were opened and they recognized him, and he disappeared from their sight.
They asked each other, "Were not our hearts burning within us while he talked with us on the road and opened the Scriptures to us? Luke 24:30-32.

Every form of the mental block should be cleared forever in Jesus' name.

The stew was poured out for the men, but as they began to eat it, they cried out, "Man of God, there is death in the pot!" And they could not eat it.
Elisha said, "Get some flour." He put it into the pot and said, "Serve it to the people to eat." And there was nothing harmful in the pot. 2 King 4:40-41

Communion is prescribed for every poison in our system to be neutralized.

For whenever you eat this bread and drink this cup, you proclaim the Lord's death until he comes. 1 Corinthians 11:26

The Communion is prescribed for Health, Strength, and Longevity:

That is why many among you are weak and sick, and a number of you have fallen asleep. 1 Corinthians 11:30

BLOOD OF JESUS FOR HEALING

The Blood brings Life and Healing
For the life of the flesh is in the blood, and I have given it to you upon the altar to make atonement for your souls; for it is the blood that makes atonement for the soul. Lev 17:11

But He was wounded for our transgressions, He was bruised for our iniquities; the chastisement for our peace was upon Him, and by His stripes we were healed. Isaiah 53:5

But if Christ is in you, your body is dead because of sin, yet your spirit is alive because of righteousness.
And if the Spirit of him who raised Jesus from the dead is living in you, he who raised Christ from the dead will also give life to your mortal bodies through his Spirit, who lives in you. Romans 8:10-11

In this chapter, we examine how the Blood of Jesus can bring healing to our bodies.
Romans 8:1-21Therefore, there is now no condemnation for those who are in Christ Jesus, 2 because through Christ Jesus the law of the Spirit of life set me free from the law of sin and death.

Passover and Communion
The Passover meal (recorded in Ex. 12:1-14) was a type of Communion, and it was first celebrated on the night in which the deliverance of the people of God from the servitude of Egypt took place. The Passover experience was and is symbolic of several things.

Deliverance: The exodus of the Israelites from Egypt represents their deliverance wrought (created and formed) by Christ—who is the "Lamb slain from the foundation of the world" (Rev. 13:8), as part of the atoning work of Jesus. Their deliverance from Egypt was both spiritual and physical.
Lamb: The lamb without blemish that was slain was a shadow and type of the (then yet-to-be) crucifixion of Jesus. The Israelites

were to have the "lamb" in them, as well as the "blood" over them.

Blood: The blood on the doorposts represents the blood spilt by Jesus on Calvary for the remission of sins and our salvation.
Readiness: The eating of the Passover meal "with your loins girded, your shoes on your feet, and your staff in your hand" (Ex. 12:11) was symbolic of God's continual and universal desire to lead his people out of bondage and into new life.
Blood on the Doorposts: The blood on the doorposts represented God's protection from the oncoming angel of death.

Unleavened Bread: The eating of unleavened bread represented their charge to leave sin behind (refer also to Mat. 16:11-12, regarding the leaven—or false "doctrine"—of the Pharisees and the Sadducees).

Provision: The "spoils" of Egypt were given to the Israelites as a symbol of God's all-embracing provision for them (Gen. 12:35-36).

Healing: "There was not one feeble person" among the 2 or 3 million Israelites (Ps. 105:37) who departed with Moses. This occurrence is symbolic of God's power and promises to heal our bodies. "But if the Spirit of him that raised Jesus from the dead dwell in you, he that raised Christ from the dead shall also quicken your mortal bodies by his Spirit that dwelleth in you" (Rom. 8:11). Our mortal bodies are quickened (enlivened) as we remember and celebrate Communion.

Celebration: The Passover meal was a time of celebration, a feast —a time to celebrate victory (not to shed or remember the tears of the past). Wine is also a symbol of celebration. Communion is to be celebrated as a joyous meal. We should come to this celebration rejoicing.
Memorial: God commanded the Israelites to keep the Passover Feast as a memorial and ordinance forever (Ex. 12:14). The Passover Feast was to be a time of remembrance; its celebration is to be a memorial of the burial and resurrection of our Lord.

Proclamation: The Passover event was a proclamation to the enemies of God and the devil, that God will lead His people. It was also an occasion of defeat for the devil.
Communion: Communion suggests a family gathering around the Holy Table. As Jesus portrayed it, He and His disciples fellowshipped together as the family of God. Everyone had (and has) the same access to the Table. All were invited to come to the Passover meal with Jesus, even Judas.

As with the Passover Feast, coming to the Communion Table should include an appropriation of deliverance from the powers of sin and death and an appropriation of physical strength, healing, and provision through expectant faith—by consumption of the (bread) body of the Lord, through whose stripes we are healed. To leave the Table without asking for (and appropriating) both spiritual and physical blessing is to neglect the provisions offered through the atoning death of Christ.
John 6 speaks of Jesus Himself as "the living bread" that has come down from heaven. This acknowledgement was in contrast to the bread that Israel was fed in the wilderness. Their "manna" (bread) physically sustained the whole nation for their entire journey of over 40 years. We may have confidence, then, that the living bread from heaven (of which the manna was a type) is given to sustain us, both physically and spiritually. We should therefore come to the Table with a confident expectation of physical strength, forgiveness and healing. This passage in John 6 also states, "He that eateth my flesh, and drinketh my blood, dwelleth in me, and I in him" (vs. 56). When we partake of the emblems, we do so with the assurance that Jesus is abiding in us.
Mat. 15:22-28 speaks of the "children's bread." Bread is the most basic necessity of human existence. To deny someone bread is to deny them the very staff of life. In this instance, calling healing the "children's bread," Jesus was declaring that healing is the most basic provision of the Father. Interesting it is, indeed, that Jesus also asked, "If a son shall ask bread of any of you that is a father,

will he give him a stone?" (Luke 11:12, Mat. 7:9). In petitioning our Heavenly Father for healing, we should have confidence that it is His delight to give us what we ask for.

In approaching the Table of the Lord, we have two things which are relevant to healing: (1) Jesus is the living bread from heaven, imparting His divine life to us by the Spirit, and (2) the bread as the "children's bread"—meaning healing itself.

A study of "blood" in the old testament will aid in the understanding of its significance. Victory over Satan requires entering into and remaining in the blood of Jesus. The Cross is the only place the blood of Jesus was poured out for us. The Blood receives its authentic power and has an effect when we come in true repentance to the Cross and remain there.

Blood is the power that releases the power of the Almighty and opens the heavens and manifests the glory of God. The blood is the door through which we enter to be united with God. It is where the Spirit of God and the spirit of man merge. The Blood of Jesus is the way through which we can approach the throne of grace.

The Table is, first, a place of intimacy where we can experience the presence of the Lord through the power of the Holy Spirit. We can fully expect Jesus to manifest His presence at the Table, and this should be our primary focus. As we feast upon the bread, by faith —we receive the life and strength of God through the Spirit. As the bread in the wilderness fed Israel day by day, giving them physical sustenance, so Jesus, the living bread from heaven, imparts to us spiritual, emotional, and physical strength. He comes to impart those things made freely available through His sacrificial death.

As we partake of the wine, the symbol of life itself, and the life that Jesus poured out for us, we become united with Him, which is a type of "blood covenant" that can protect us from evil and lays the basis for His claim upon us to be a part of His kingdom on this earth, as well as in heaven because of His sacrifice and His resurrection.

We must come to the Table with sufficient preparation, having made an honest evaluation of ourselves before God. Besides admonishing us to examine ourselves before partaking, 1 Corinthians 11:23-31 links being "weak and sickly" to our unworthiness, to our lack of understanding of how we worthily approach the Table and the body and blood of our Lord (where there is great healing power in the partaking of Communion once faith and understanding are made sufficient.

Communion is the holiest sacrament, a sacred ceremony involving symbols of Christ's sacrifice and our covenant—to signify a spiritual bond between God and mankind. We always have the choice to choose God or mammon. In Genesis 14:18-20, Abraham chose to pay his tithes and be served bread and wine, rather than to keep the spoils of the King of Sodom.

In preparation for Jewish marriage, after the fathers have negotiated the bride price (the price the groom agrees to pay for the father's loss of his daughter), the groom offers a cup to the woman asking, "I love you and give you my life. Will you marry me?" If the woman drinks from the cup, she is—in essence—saying, "Yes, I will marry you." Jesus, likewise, as He raised His cup to His disciples (and as He continues to offer His cup to us today), was asking that they join Him in covenant—to be His bride (the body), as is stated: "And he took the cup, and when he had given thanks, he gave it to them: and they all drank of it. And he said unto them, This is my blood of the new testament, which is shed for many" (Mark 14:22-24, Mat. 26:26-28, Luke 22:19-20).

At the Table we are made one body and one flesh with Christ. He is the bread of life and the source of the living water. Those who come to Him will never hunger or thirst. To eat the bread representing the body of the Lord Jesus and to drink the wine of Communion implies the appropriation of everything Christ's body and blood represents. It is the very essence of His magnificence. It is the greatest revelation of His love for men. It is both the life force drained from His body at the crucifixion and the blood that flowed again through his resurrected body.

Communion is His gift of Himself.
The Table is a place to receive forgiveness. The wine speaks to us of His blood, shed for the remission of sins. His blood opened a "new and living way" into the Father's presence. Communion also offers us an opportunity to receive forgiveness and healing for our family tree, although this practice is not commonly observed; completed genograms are presented for the healing and blessing of our spiritual inheritance. While partaking of Communion in this effort, powerful healing occurs and many are thereby freed from the adverse generational influences of the past. (Refer to the section on "Healing from Generational Influences" for additional insight on this subject.) If possible, communion should be shared appropriately with every seeker who comes for prayer for deliverance and inner healing.

Pray for the Following at the Communion table.
For forgiveness
For the release of forgiveness of others toward us (We can bind others with un-forgiveness, and they can bind us; this is the releasing of the "they can bind us" part of the spiritual law of binding and losing.)
For the covenant benefits of Jesus' death and resurrection
For our portion of the "children's bread" of healing
For physical healing, health, and strength
For protection from the angel of death
That Jesus may abide within us
For His mercy and kindness
For provision

Prayer
Lord, we know that this Communion represents an opportunity for the closest possible connection with Jesus, as it represents both a spiritual and a physical encounter with our Lord. We know that the scriptures tell us, "He that eateth my flesh, and drinketh my blood, dwelleth in me, and I in him."
By partaking in this bread and wine, we are consuming spiritual

food and are made "one body" and "one flesh" in Christ Jesus. These symbols are a most precious and special gift to yourself. You are the bread of life and the living water. Your broken body has provided for our physical health and healing. Your spilt blood has provided for us forgiveness and spiritual healing.

Lord, we come today desiring to receive healing of our spirits as well as of our bodies and to remember our covenant with you which we made in the waters of baptism. By this act of faith, we appropriate the blood of Jesus that was shed for us, and we pray that the full power of this Communion is applied to us and our families.

We thank you, Lord Jesus, for these blessings, offered in your most precious name Amen.

www.ingramcontent.com/pod-product-compliance
Lightning Source LLC
LaVergne TN
LVHW050347160826
845677LV00014B/3844

* 9 7 9 8 8 4 0 2 0 8 1 9 9 *